Day 1

Can a rock grow?

WEEK 1

Some things **grow**, and some things do not.

Vocabulary

grow
to get bigger

1. What do you think can grow?
Circle your guesses.

2. Complete the sentence. Write the word.

Some things 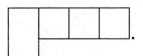 .

3. What grows and changes at your home?
Write the word. Draw a picture of it.

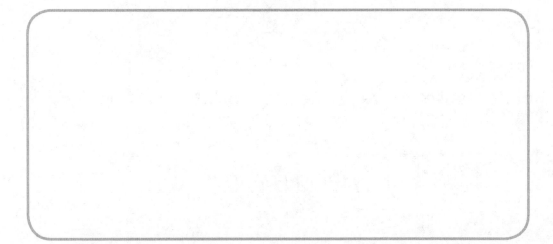

Day 2

Weekly Question
Can a rock grow?

Daily Science

Big Idea 1

WEEK 1

Only **living** things can grow.
An animal is a living thing.
A plant is a living thing.
Living things grow and change.

Vocabulary

living
having life

1. What does each living thing grow into?
   Draw lines to match.

   •   •

   •   •

   •   •

2. Complete the sentence. Write the word.

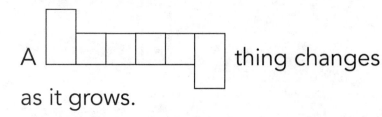

A ☐☐☐☐☐☐ thing changes

as it grows.

2

Daily Science • EMC 6871 • © Evan-Moor Corp.

Day 3

Living things need food, water, and air. These help living things **survive**. Food, water, and air also help living things grow and change.

Vocabulary

survive
to stay living

1. Complete the sentence. Write the word.

Living things need **food**, **water**,

and **air** to ⬚⬚⬚⬚⬚⬚⬚.

2. Read each sentence. Circle **yes** or **no**.

A cat needs food to survive.   yes   no

A tree needs air to survive.   yes   no

A baby needs toys to survive.   yes   no

3. Color the things a dog needs to survive.

  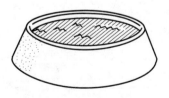

food   ball   water

Day 4

Weekly Question

Can a rock grow?

Daily Science

Big Idea 1

WEEK 1

A rock is **nonliving**. It does not grow and change. It does not need food, water, or air.

Vocabulary

nonliving
not having life

1. Put an **X** on the nonliving things.

2. How are all nonliving things alike?
Fill in the bubble next to the correct answer.

Ⓐ They don't need food, water, or air.

Ⓑ They move and breathe.

Ⓒ They grow and change.

3. List four nonliving things in your classroom.

_____   _____

_____   _____

4. Complete the sentence. Write the word.

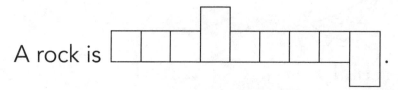

A rock is

4

Weekly Question
Can a rock grow?

1. Color the picture of a living thing.

Teddy Bear	Big Bear

2. Look at the bears again. Circle **yes** or **no**.

Teddy Bear grows.   yes   no

Big Bear is living.   yes   no

Big Bear eats.   yes   no

3. Complete the sentences. Use the words in the box.

> living   nonliving   survive

A rock is _____.

A butterfly is _____.

I need air, water, and food to _____.

Day 1

Weekly Question

Do monkeys really eat bananas?

Living things eat food to get **energy**.

1. Draw a line from each animal to a food it eats for energy.

 •

 •

 •

 •

• bananas

• grass

• fish

• worms

Vocabulary

energy
the power to do work

2. Complete each sentence. Write the word.

Monkeys eat to get ☐☐☐☐☐☐ .

We eat to get ☐☐☐☐☐☐ .

Day 2

Do monkeys really eat bananas?

People eat many kinds of food to get energy.

1. Circle the things people eat.

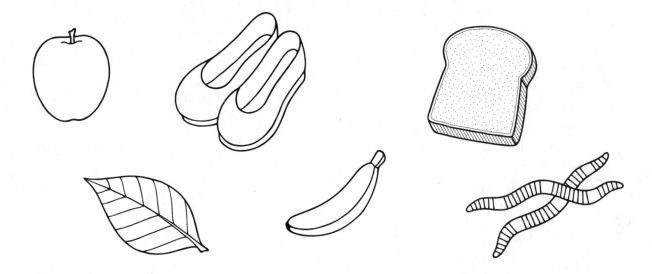

2. Draw a picture of what you eat to get energy.
Then complete the sentence about it.

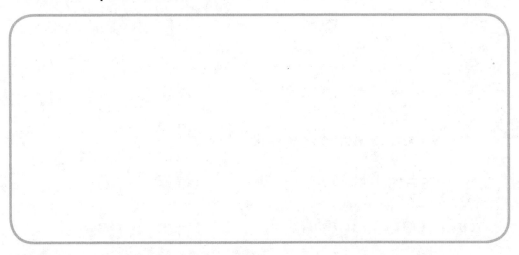

I eat _____ to get energy.

Day 3 *Weekly Question*
Do monkeys really eat bananas?

Animals need food to get energy. They eat food that grows where they live.

1. Draw lines to match the animals with where they get their food.

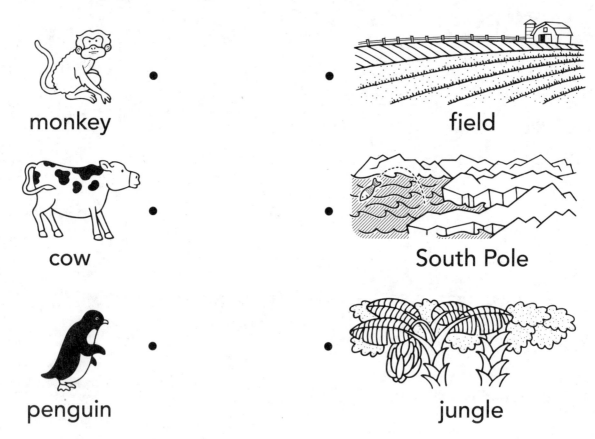

monkey   •   •   field

cow   •   •   South Pole

penguin   •   •   jungle

2. Read each sentence. Circle **yes** or **no**.

A monkey eats fish.   yes   no

A penguin eats bananas.   yes   no

A cow eats grass.   yes   no

Day 4

Do monkeys really eat bananas?

Daily Science

Big Idea 1

WEEK 2

Animals eat food that is easy to get.

Circle the food that is easy for each animal to get.

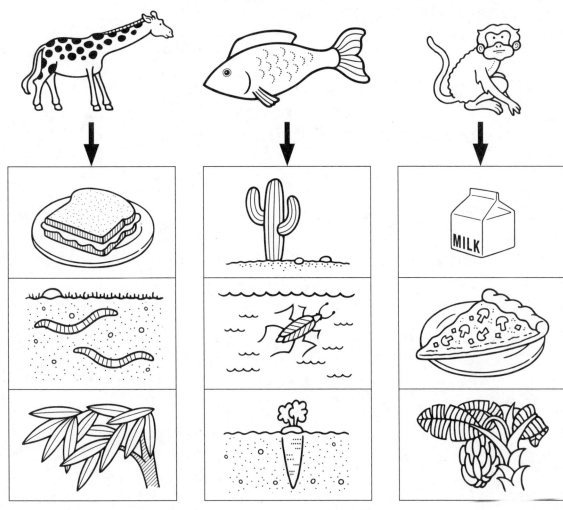

 Talk

Discuss with your partner what you like to eat every day.

Weekly Question
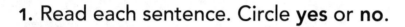

Do monkeys really eat bananas?

1. Read each sentence. Circle **yes** or **no**.

Animals need food to live.	yes	no
Animals eat food that grows where they live.	yes	no
All animals can eat anything.	yes	no
People eat food to get energy.	yes	no

2. Draw a picture of each thing.

Something you eat	Something a monkey eats

3. Read the question. Circle **yes** or **no**.

Do monkeys eat bananas?   yes   no

Day 1

Weekly Question

Do plants have mouths?

Daily Science

Big Idea 1

WEEK 3

Plants make their own food. They need air, light, and water to make food.

1. Draw lines from the plant to the things it needs to make food.

2. Complete the sentence. Write the word.

A plant uses air, light, and water to make 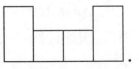.

Do plants have mouths?

Plants have different parts. They have **leaves**, **roots**, and **stems**. The parts have jobs to do. They help the plant make food.

1. Name the parts of the plant. Write the words.

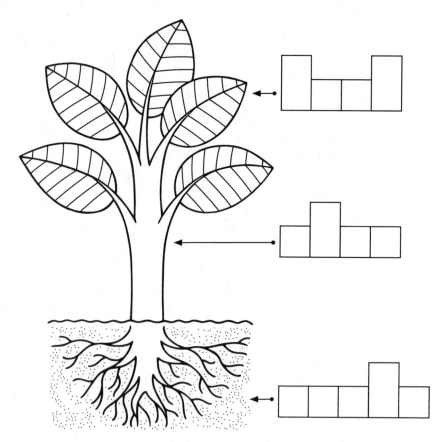

Vocabulary

leaf
the part of a plant that gets sunlight and makes food

roots
the parts of a plant under the ground that get water

stem
the main part of a plant that moves and stores food and water

2. Color the plant above.
Color the leaves and stem green.
Color the roots brown.

Day 3

Weekly Question

Do plants have mouths?

Plants do not have mouths. But plants eat.
Plants use their leaves to make food.
Plants use their roots to get water.

1. Look at the picture. Complete each sentence.

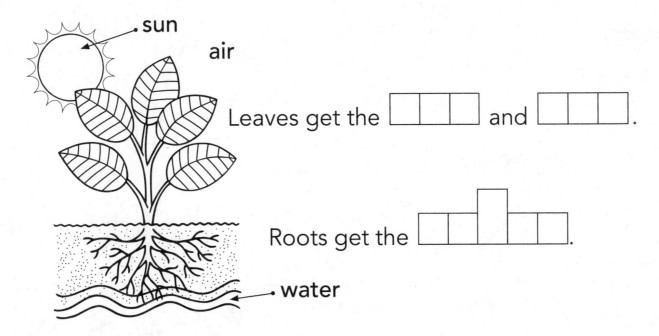

sun

air

Leaves get the ☐☐☐ and ☐☐☐.

Roots get the ☐☐☐☐☐.

water

2. Read each sentence. Circle **yes** or **no**.

A leaf gets water.	yes	no
A leaf gets sun.	yes	no
Roots get water.	yes	no

Day 4

Weekly Question
Do plants have mouths?

Plants use their stems to move food and water.
Water moves from the roots up the stem.
Food moves from the leaves down the stem.

1. Color the food blocks green.
   Color the water drops blue.
   Complete the sentence.

Leaves make **food**.

Stems move the _____

and the _____.

Roots get **water**.

2. Complete each sentence. Write the word **stem**.

Water goes up the ⬚⬚⬚.

Food goes down the ⬚⬚⬚.

Weekly Question

Do plants have mouths?

Circle the answers.

1. What do plants need to make food?

2. What part of the plant makes food?

3. What part of the plant gets water?

 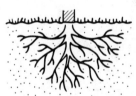 

4. What part of the plant moves the food and water?

 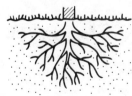

5. Do plants have mouths?   yes   no

Day 1 *Weekly Question*
Do fish drink water?

All living things need water.

1. Circle the things that need water. Color the picture.

2. What do all these things need? Write the word.

The dog needs ⬚⬚⬚⬚⬚.

The fish needs ⬚⬚⬚⬚⬚.

The plant needs ⬚⬚⬚⬚⬚.

Daily Science • EMC 6871 • © Evan-Moor Corp.

Day 2

Weekly Question
Do fish drink water?

Some fish live in **fresh water**. A lake and a river are fresh water. Some fish live in **salt water**. The ocean is salt water.

Draw a fish in each picture. Then write the word to complete each sentence.

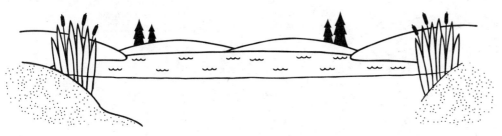

A lake and a river are ☐☐☐☐ water.

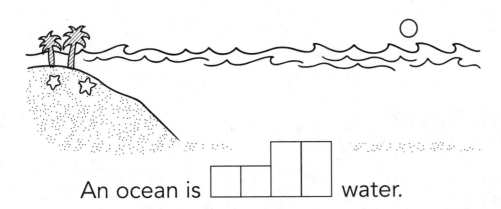

An ocean is ☐☐☐ water.

Vocabulary

fresh water
water without a lot of salt; lakes and rivers are fresh water

salt water
water with a lot of salt; oceans are salt water

 Talk

What bodies of water are near you? Are they fresh water or salt water? Talk about it with your partner.

Day 3

Weekly Question
Do fish drink water?

All fish have **gills**. Fish that live in fresh water use their gills to get water.

1. What does a fish use to get water?
   Write the word. Color the fish.

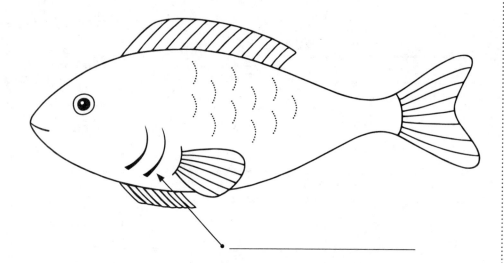

_____

2. Complete the sentences. Write the words.

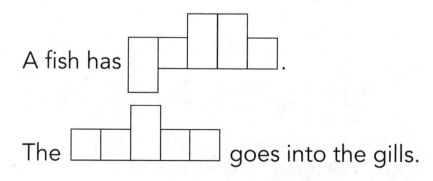

A fish has ⬚⬚⬚ .

The ⬚⬚⬚⬚⬚ goes into the gills.

Day 4

Weekly Question
Do fish drink water?

Daily Science
Big Idea 1
WEEK 4

Fish that live in salt water drink with their **mouths**. The water has lots of salt. The salt goes out the fish's gills.

Vocabulary

mouth
the part of a saltwater fish that gets water

1. Write the parts of the fish.

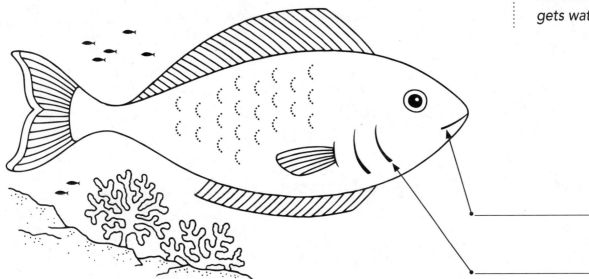

2. Complete the sentences. Write the words.

Water goes into the fish's 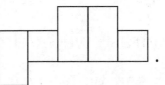 .

The salt comes out of the ⬚⬚⬚ .

© Evan-Moor Corp. • EMC 6871 • *Daily Science*

19

Day 5

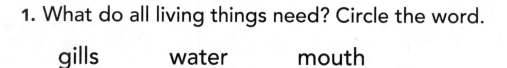

Weekly Question
Do fish drink water?

1. What do all living things need? Circle the word.

gills   water   mouth

2. Read each sentence. Circle **yes** or **no**.

Fish live in water.	yes	no
Fish use gills to eat.	yes	no
A river has salt water.	yes	no
The ocean has salt water.	yes	no

3. Draw the mouth and gills. Then color the fish.

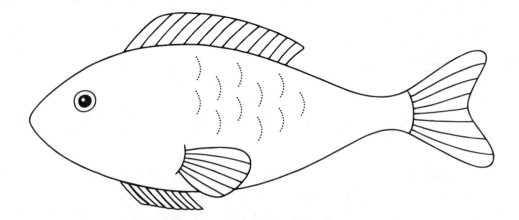

4. Read each question. Circle **yes** or **no**.

Do fish in fresh water drink with their mouths?	yes	no
Do fish in salt water drink with their mouths?	yes	no

Comprehension

Needs of Living Things

Read each question. Circle the answer.

1. Which of these is living?

2. What does a monkey eat?

3. What plant part makes food?

4. Which of these will grow?

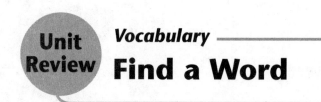

Read each riddle. Circle the correct word.

1. I am very big.   lake   ocean
   I am full of salty water.

2. We are part of a plant.   leaves   roots
   We help the plant make food.

3. I am part of a fish.   river   gills
   I help the fish get water.

4. I help you do work.   stem   energy
   You get me from food.

5. I am not like you.   living   nonliving
   I describe a rock.

6. When I do this, I change.   grow   survive
   I get bigger and taller.

Unit Review · *Visual Literacy* — **Picture This!**

1. Use the words to write the parts of the plant.

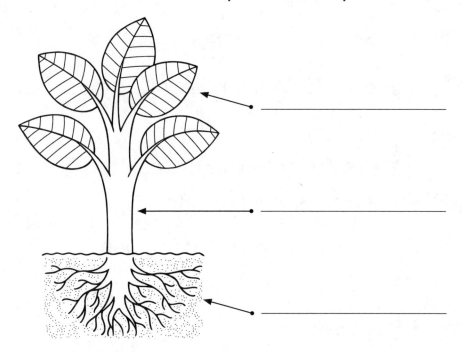

leaf

roots

stem

2. Use the words to write the parts of the fish.

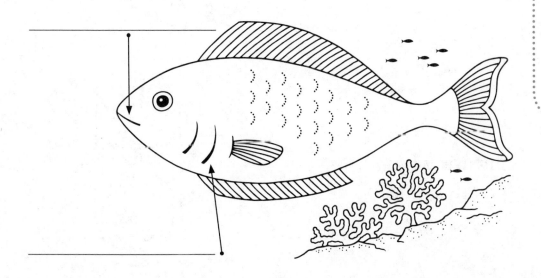

mouth

gills

WEEK 5

© Evan-Moor Corp. • EMC 6871 • *Daily Science* 23

Watch a Plant Drink!

You can see how a plant drinks water. Try this test.

What You Need

- celery stalk with leaves
- red food coloring
- glass of water
- safety scissors
- crayons

1. Stir red food coloring into the water.

2. Have an adult help you cut the bottom off the celery stalk.

3. Put the celery in the colored water. Leave it alone for a whole day.

4. Check to see what happened!

What Did You Discover?

Color the celery to show what happened.

 Talk

Tell your partner what happened to the celery.

Day 1

Daily Science

Big Idea 2

WEEK 1

A **habitat** is the place where animals live, eat, and sleep. There are many kinds of habitats on Earth.

1. Match each animal to its habitat.

owl

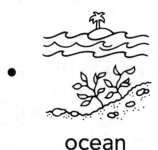

ocean

fish

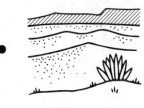

desert

camel

forest

Vocabulary

habitat
a place where plants and animals live

2. Complete the sentence. Write the word.

All animals live in a 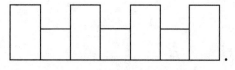 .

Day 2

Where do animals sleep?

Daily Science

Big Idea 2

WEEK 1

A **forest** is a habitat. A forest has many trees and plants. Many animals live in a forest. Some live in **nests**. Some live in **dens**. Some live in **holes**.

1. Find the forest animals. Circle them.

Vocabulary

den
a home for wild animals

forest
a land full of many trees, plants, and animals

nest
a home for birds that is usually in a tree

2. Use the picture to complete each sentence.

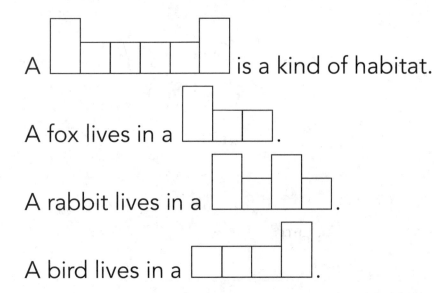

A ☐☐☐☐☐ is a kind of habitat.

A fox lives in a ☐☐☐.

A rabbit lives in a ☐☐☐☐.

A bird lives in a ☐☐☐☐.

Day 3

Where do animals sleep?

WEEK 1

A **desert** is a habitat. Deserts are very dry. They are hot in the day and cold at night. Many animals live inside rocks or under the ground. It keeps them warm at night and cool during the day.

Vocabulary

desert
a dry place with few plants and animals

1. Find the desert animals. Circle them.

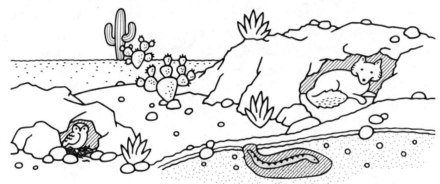

2. Complete the sentences. Write the words.

A ▢▢▢▢▢▢ is a kind of habitat.

A snake lives in a ▢▢▢.

A coyote lives in a ▢▢.

 Talk

Name one way a forest is different from a desert. Tell your partner.

Day 4

Where do animals sleep?

An **ocean** is a big body of salty water. Many ocean animals live near plants or rocks under the water. Some animals live near the top of the water.

Vocabulary

ocean
a large body of salt water that covers most of Earth

1. Find the ocean animals. Circle them.

2. Read each sentence. Circle **yes** or **no**.

A whale lives in the ocean.   **yes**   **no**

A camel lives in the ocean.   **yes**   **no**

An octopus lives in the ocean.   **yes**   **no**

Where do animals sleep?

1. Complete each sentence. Fill in the bubble next to the correct word.

A fox sleeps in a den in the _____.

Ⓐ forest   Ⓑ bedroom   Ⓒ ocean

Only a few animals and plants live in the _____.

Ⓐ ocean   Ⓑ desert   Ⓒ forest

2. Write the name of each habitat.
   Use the words in the box.

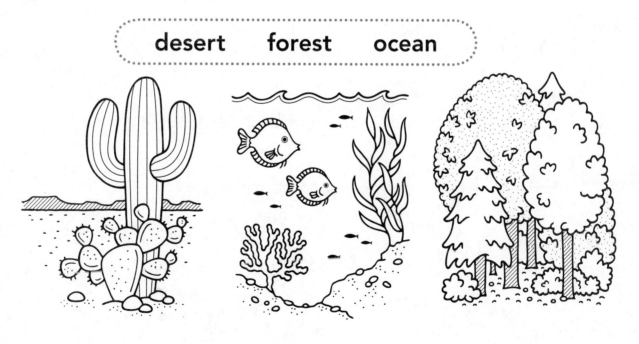

desert   forest   ocean

_____   _____   _____

Day 1

Weekly Question
Why do camels have humps?

A **camel** lives in the **desert**. The desert is hot and dry. There is not much food or water.

1. Which animal lives in the desert? Circle the animal.

2. Complete each sentence. Write the word.

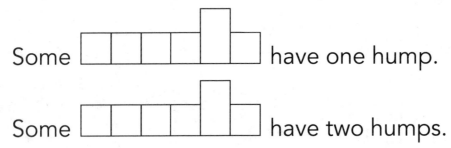

Some ⬚⬚⬚⬚⬚ have one hump.

Some ⬚⬚⬚⬚⬚ have two humps.

3. Write how many humps each camel has.

_____ _____

Vocabulary

camel
a large animal that lives in the desert and has a hump

Day 2

Weekly Question
Why do camels have humps?

It does not rain much in the desert. Few plants grow. Animals must look hard for food and water. Sometimes it is far away.

1. Help the camel find food and water. Draw a line.

2. Complete the sentence. Write the words.

A camel must look for ☐☐☐ and ☐☐☐ .

 Talk

What would you take to the desert? Tell your partner.

Day 3

Weekly Question
Why do camels have humps?

WEEK 2

A camel **stores** fat in its hump. The fat helps the camel go without food for a long time.

1. Write the word. Then color the camel.

The hump 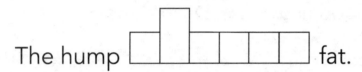 fat.

Vocabulary

stores
keeps or saves for later

2. Complete the sentences. Use the words in the box.

> desert   hump   stores

A camel has a _____ made of fat.

Humps help camels live in the _____.

The hump _____ fat.

Day 4

Why do camels have humps?

Daily Science

Big Idea 2

WEEK 2

A camel has other body parts that help it live in the desert. A camel has **big feet** to help it walk in sand. A camel has **long eyelashes** to keep sand out of its eyes.

1. Name the body parts. Trace the words.

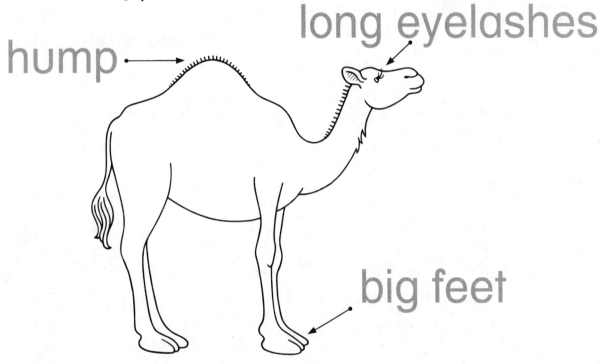

long eyelashes

hump

big feet

2. Read about camels. Circle **yes** or **no**.

A camel's big feet help it swim.	yes	no
Long eyelashes keep sand out of its eyes.	yes	no
A camel's big feet help it walk in the sand.	yes	no

Day 5

Weekly Question
Why do camels have humps?

Daily Science

Big Idea 2

WEEK 2

1. Read the sentences. Circle **yes** or **no**.

It rains a lot in the desert.   yes   no

Food is hard to find in
the desert.   yes   no

A camel's hump helps it
live in the desert.   yes   no

2. Complete the sentences. Use the words in the box.

> feet   camel   water   fat

It is hard to find ⬚⬚⬚⬚ in the desert.

A ⬚⬚⬚⬚ has long eyelashes.

A camel's hump is made of ⬚⬚⬚.

A camel's big ⬚⬚⬚⬚ help it walk in sand.

Day 1

Weekly Question

Can a whale live in a lake?

The **ocean** is very big. It is full of salty water. Lots of plants live in the ocean. Lots of animals live there, too. A **whale** lives in the ocean. A whale is very big.

Vocabulary

whale
a large animal that lives in the ocean and breathes air

1. Trace the words. Then color the picture.

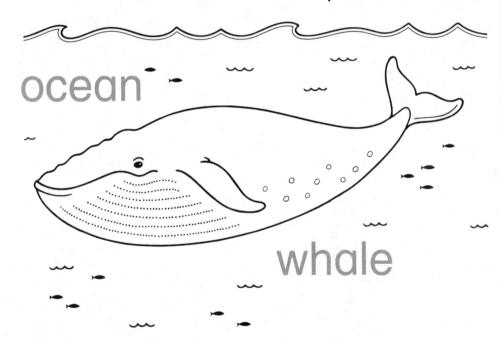

2. Complete the sentences. Use the words from the picture.

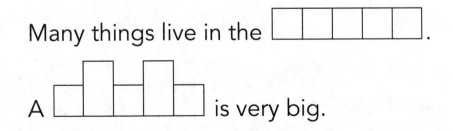

Many things live in the ☐☐☐☐☐.

A ☐☐☐☐☐ is very big.

Day 2

Weekly Question

Can a whale live in a lake?

Daily Science

Big Idea 2

WEEK 3

A whale is the biggest animal in the ocean. Many whales eat **krill**. Krill are very small animals. They look like shrimp. Krill live in the ocean.

Vocabulary

krill
a very small animal that looks like a shrimp

1. What is the whale eating? Write the word.

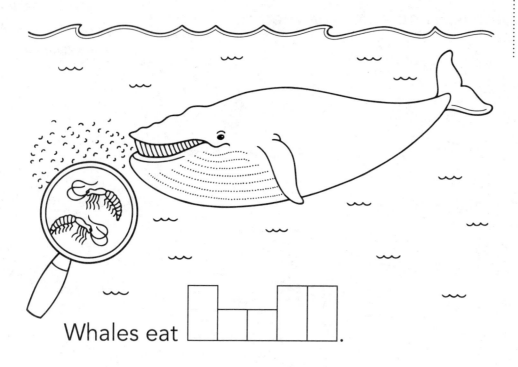

Whales eat ⬚⬚⬚⬚⬚.

2. Read each sentence. Circle yes or no.

Krill are bigger than whales.   yes   no

Whales eat krill.   yes   no

Whales and krill both live in water.   yes   no

Krill are a kind of plant.   yes   no

Daily Science • EMC 6871 • © Evan-Moor Corp.

Weekly Question

Can a whale live in a lake?

A **lake** is not like an ocean. A lake is much smaller than an ocean. The water in a lake is not salty. Plants and animals live in a lake. But they are different from the animals that live in an ocean.

Vocabulary

lake
a body of fresh water that is smaller than an ocean

1. Circle the animals in the lake. Complete the sentence. Then color the picture.

Many animals live in a ☐☐☐ .

2. Read each sentence. Circle **yes** or **no**.

   Water in a lake is salty.   yes   no

   A lake is smaller than an ocean.   yes   no

   Only plants live in a lake.   yes   no

Day 4

Can a whale live in a lake?

Daily Science

Big Idea 2

WEEK 3

A whale cannot live in a **lake**. A lake is too small. A lake does not have the right food for a whale. A whale lives in the **ocean**.

Tell what each picture shows. Write **lake** or **ocean**. Then draw a whale in the place where it lives.

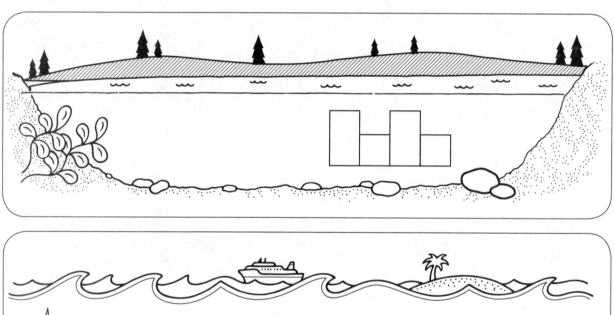

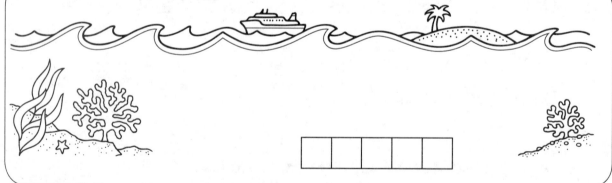

 Talk

How is a lake different from an ocean? How are they the same? Talk about it with a partner.

Weekly Question

Can a whale live in a lake?

Daily Science

Big Idea 2

WEEK 3

1. Complete the sentences. Circle the correct words.

Whales live in the ____.

   lake   ocean   river

The ocean has ____.

   salt water   fresh water

A lake is too small for a ____.

   fish   whale

2. Complete the sentences. Use the words in the box.

> krill   lake   whale

A _____ is the biggest animal in the ocean.

Many whales eat _____.

A whale cannot live in a _____.

Weekly Question

Day 1

Why do trees have different kinds of leaves?

Big Idea 2

WEEK 4

All trees have **leaves**. The leaves have many different shapes.

1. Trace the leaves.

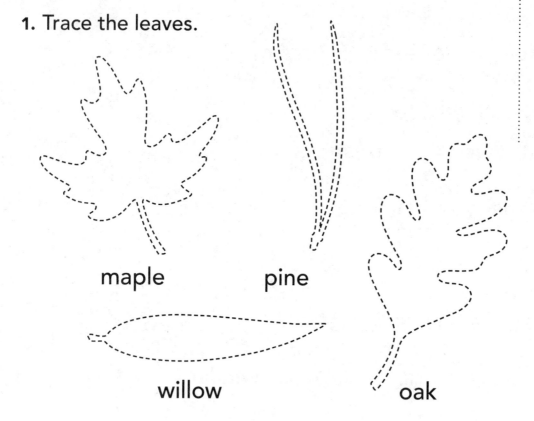

maple

pine

willow

oak

Vocabulary

leaves
the parts of a plant or tree that take in light and air to make food

2. Complete the sentence. Write the word.

There are many kinds of ☐☐☐☐☐☐.

 Talk

What kinds of leaves do you see where you live?

Daily Science • EMC 6871 • © Evan-Moor Corp.

Day 2

Why do trees have different kinds of leaves?

Daily Science

Big Idea 2

WEEK 4

Some trees have flat leaves. They live in places that are warm in the summer and cold in the winter. The flat leaves soak up the sun. In the spring and summer, the leaves are green. In the fall, the leaves turn red, yellow, and orange.

1. Color the leaves in the summer.
   Color the leaves in the fall.

Summer   **Fall**

2. Complete the sentences. Write the words.

> **green   red**

Leaves are ⬚⬚⬚⬚⬚ in the summer.

Some leaves turn ⬚⬚⬚ in the fall.

Day 3

Why do trees have different kinds of leaves?

Daily Science

Big Idea 2

WEEK 4

An **evergreen** tree grows in cold places. It has thin, pointy leaves that look like needles. The leaves stay green all year. They store food and water.

Vocabulary

evergreen
a tree with short or long, thin leaves that stay green all year

1. Color the picture.

2. Complete each sentence. Use the words in the box.

> cold   leaves   trees

There are many tall evergreen _____.

The trees have pointy _____.

It is _____ in the forest.

    Daily Science • EMC 6871 • © Evan-Moor Corp.

Why do trees have different kinds of leaves?

Evergreen trees keep their leaves all year long. The leaves are strong. They do not blow off. Trees with flat leaves lose their leaves in the winter. The leaves dry up and fall off.

1. Match the tree in the summer to the same tree in the winter. Color the trees.

Summer	Winter

2. Read each sentence. Circle **yes** or **no**.

Evergreen trees keep their leaves
all year long.   yes   no

Trees with flat leaves lose their
leaves in the summer.   yes   no

Day 5

Weekly Question

Why do trees have different kinds of leaves?

Daily Science

Big Idea 2

WEEK 4

1. Circle the leaves that turn colors in the fall. Draw a box around the leaves that stay green all year.

maple

pine

willow

oak

2. Complete each sentence. Use the words in the box.

> evergreen   leaves   winter

The _____ on trees have many different shapes.

Trees with flat leaves lose their leaves in _____.

An _____ tree has pointy leaves.

3. Circle the correct answer.

Trees have different kinds of leaves because of where the trees live.   **yes   no**

44

Daily Science • EMC 6871 • © Evan-Moor Corp.

Unit Review

Comprehension

Habitats

Daily Science

Big Idea 2

WEEK 5

Read each question. Fill in the bubble next to the correct answer.

1. Which one lives in the desert?

Ⓐ whale

Ⓑ evergreen

Ⓒ camel

2. Which one is a habitat?

Ⓐ ocean

Ⓑ fox

Ⓒ nest

3. Where can a whale live?

Ⓐ lake

Ⓑ ocean

Ⓒ forest

4. Which trees stay green through the cold winter?

Ⓐ trees with flat leaves

Ⓑ trees with no leaves

Ⓒ trees with leaves like needles

Unit Review · *Vocabulary*

Word Sort

1. Write each word in the correct list.

> forest   camel   ocean
>
> den   lake   whale
>
> desert   krill   nest

Habitats	Animals	Animal homes
_____	_____	_____
_____	_____	_____
_____		
_____		

2. Complete the sentences. Use the words in the box.

> evergreen   stores   habitat   leaves

A _____ is where an animal lives.

A camel _____ fat in its hump.

An _____ tree stays green during winter.

Some trees lose their _____ in the winter.

Visual Literacy

Picture the Habitat

1. Look at the habitat below. What is it called? Circle your answer.

    desert   forest   ocean

2. How many animals can you find? Circle and color them.

A scientist looks closely at things. Look closely at a leaf. Use the questions to help you. Then draw and label what you learn.

What You Need

- a leaf
- a hand lens
- crayons

1. Touch the leaf. Is it rough or smooth?

   _____

2. Listen. What sounds can you make

   with your leaf? _____

3. Smell. What does your leaf smell like?

   _____

4. Can you find lines, bumps, or holes?

   _____

Use crayons to make a rubbing of your leaf.

Daily Science • EMC 6871 • © Evan-Moor Corp.

What causes day and night?

Earth spins all the way around, or **rotates**, once every day. Each day, the sun and moon seem to move across the sky. But they are not moving. Earth is!

Vocabulary

Earth
the planet we live on

rotates
spins around

1. Complete the sentence about the picture.

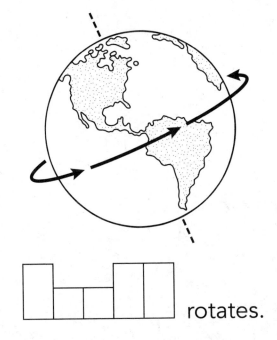

rotates.

2. Complete each sentence. Write the word.

Every 24 hours, Earth ☐☐☐☐☐.

Every time the Earth ☐☐☐☐☐, we have a new day.

Day 2

Weekly Question
What causes day and night?

Daily Science

Big Idea 3

WEEK 1

As Earth rotates, the side we live on turns toward the sun. We see the sun. It is **day**.

1. Look at the picture. Complete the sentence.

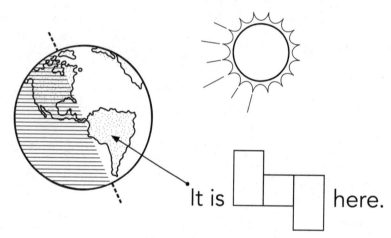

It is ☐☐ here.

2. Color the sun at each time of day.

morning   noon   evening

3. Complete the sentence. Write the word.

At _____, the sun is straight over my head.

What causes day and night?

Daily Science

Big Idea 3

WEEK 1

Earth keeps **rotating** all day. The side we live on turns away from the sun. It becomes dark. It is **night**. We see the stars.

Vocabulary

night
the time after the sun sets and before it rises, when it is dark outside

1. Look at the picture. Complete the sentence.

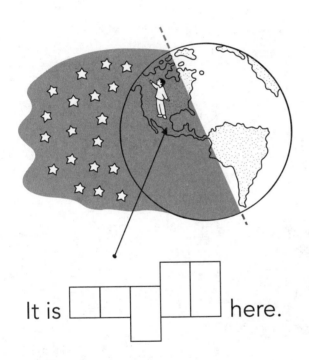

It is ☐☐☐/☐☐ here.

2. Read each sentence. Circle **yes** or **no**.

At night, our side of Earth is away from the sun.   yes   no

At night, it is dark all over Earth.   yes   no

At night, Earth stops rotating.   yes   no

© Evan-Moor Corp. • EMC 6871 • *Daily Science*

Day 4

What causes day and night?

Daily Science

Big Idea 3

WEEK 1

Earth never stops rotating. So we always have night and day!

Look at the picture. Where is it day on Earth? Where is it night? Write the words from the box.

day   night

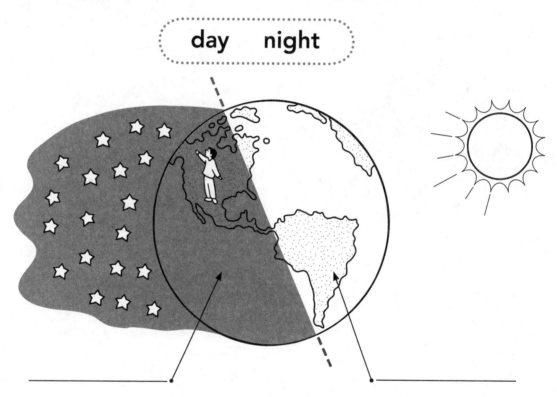

🗣️ **Talk**

If it is day where you live, what do you think it is like on the other side of Earth? Why?

Day 5

What causes day and night?

Daily Science

Big Idea 3

WEEK 1

1. Look at the picture. Then complete the sentences. Write the words.

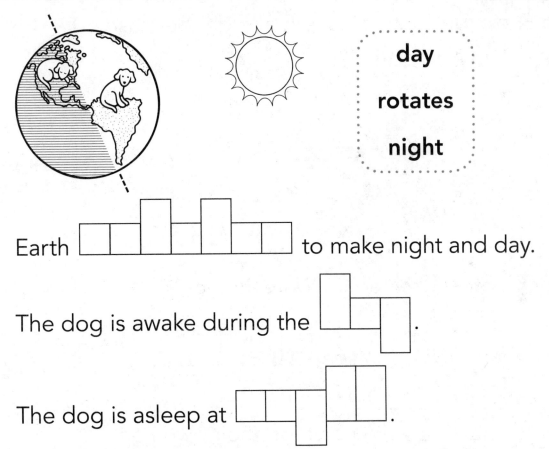

day

rotates

night

Earth ☐☐☐☐☐☐☐ to make night and day.

The dog is awake during the ☐☐☐.

The dog is asleep at ☐☐☐☐.

2. Complete the sentences. Use the words from above.

The Earth _____ like a spinning top.

When light from the sun hits Earth, it is _____.

During the _____, we are on the other side.

This is what causes day and night!

Day 1

Weekly Question

What do we see in the sky at night?

We see **stars** shining at night. Stars give off their own light. The **sun** is a star. It is the closest star to Earth. But we can't see it at night because we are facing away from it.

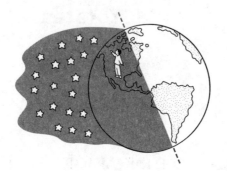

Vocabulary

stars
objects in the sky that give off light

sun
the star closest to Earth

1. Complete the sentences. Write the words.

At night, you can see ⬜⬜⬜⬜⬜ .

All ⬜⬜⬜⬜⬜ give off their own light.

The ⬜⬜⬜⬜ are very far from Earth.

Our ⬜⬜⬜ is a star.

2. Complete the rhyme.

The nearest star is really very _____ .

Day 2

Weekly Question

What do we see in the sky at night?

We see the **moon** shining at night. It is made from rock. It does not make its own light. Light from the sun makes the moon shine bright.

1. Complete the sentence. Write the word.

We see the ⬜⬜⬜⬜ in the sky.

2. Complete the sentences. Circle the correct words.

The moon is made of ____.

light   cheese   rock

The moon gets light from ____.

Earth   the sun   people

Vocabulary

moon
a large object near Earth that is made from rock and gets light from the sun

Weekly Question

Day 3

What do we see in the sky at night?

Sometimes you can see **planets** in the night sky. They do not make their own light. But light from the sun makes them bright. The closest planets to Earth are Mars and Venus.

Vocabulary

planet
a large object in space that does not make its own light

1. Complete each sentence. Write the word.

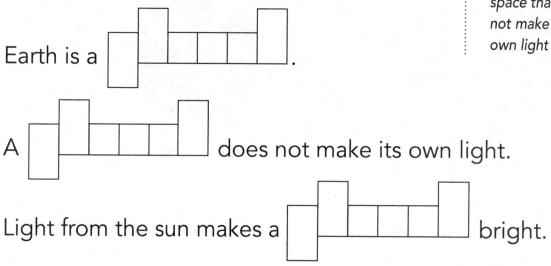

Earth is a ⬜⬜⬜⬜⬜ .

A ⬜⬜⬜⬜⬜ does not make its own light.

Light from the sun makes a ⬜⬜⬜⬜⬜ bright.

2. Color Venus brown. Color Earth blue and green. Color Mars red.

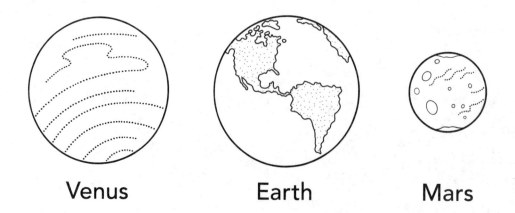

Venus   Earth   Mars

Day 4

Weekly Question

What do we see in the sky at night?

Daily Science

Big Idea 3

WEEK 2

At night, you can see stars. But during the day, you cannot see stars. That's because the sun is so bright.

1. Answer each riddle. Circle the correct picture.

You can never see me during the day. Who am I?

stars

moon

sun

You can never see me at night. Who am I?

stars

moon

sun

2. People like to find shapes in stars. One famous shape is the Big Dipper. Connect the stars. Do you see the Big Dipper?

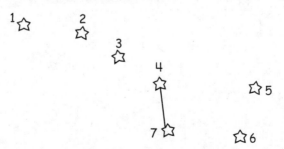

Weekly Question

Day 5

What do we see in the sky at night?

1. Answer each question. Circle **yes** or **no**.

Is Mars a planet?   yes   no

Does the moon make its
own light?   yes   no

Do we see stars at night?   yes   no

2. What do we see in the night sky? Write the words.

Day 1

Weekly Question

Why do we need the sun?

Daily Science

Big Idea 3

WEEK 3

The sun gives us **energy**. We see the energy as **light**. We feel the energy as **heat**.

Vocabulary

energy
power we can use

heat
energy we can feel

light
energy we can see

1. Complete the sentences. Write the words.

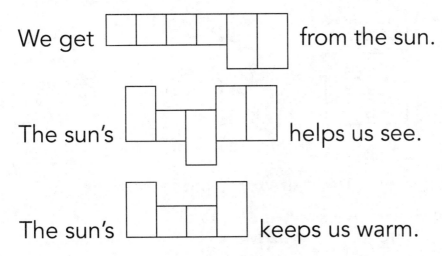

We get ☐☐☐☐☐☐ from the sun.

The sun's ☐☐☐☐☐ helps us see.

The sun's ☐☐☐☐ keeps us warm.

2. Answer the riddle. Write the word.

I give off my own light.
I give heat to Earth.
Everyone needs me.
What am I?

I am the _____.

Day 2

Weekly Question

Why do we need the sun?

The sun gives us light and heat. We need light and heat to live.

1. Circle all the things that can give us light or heat.

2. Answer the questions. Use the words in the box.

light   heat

What helps us see at night?   _____

What helps us cook our food?   _____

What do we get from fire?   _____ and

_____

Day 3

Weekly Question

Why do we need the sun?

The sun helps plants make food. Without the sun, plants would not grow. Without plants, animals and people would not have food.

1. Circle the things that need the sun.

2. Complete the sentences. Use the words in the box.

food   live   plants

Without the sun, 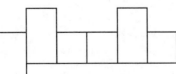 would not grow.

Without plants, we would not have 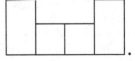.

Without the sun, we could not 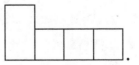.

Day 4

Why do we need the sun?

Daily Science

Big Idea 3

WEEK 3

The sun helps us live. But it is also very powerful. We must stay safe in the sun.

1. Read each sentence. Draw a line to the picture that shows what to do in the sun.

Do this so the sun doesn't burn your skin.

Do this so you don't get thirsty in the sun.

Do this so the sun doesn't hurt your eyes.

2. Read each sentence. Circle **yes** or **no**.

We could live without the sun.   yes   no

The sun is very weak.   yes   no

We must be careful in the sun.   yes   no

 Talk

What are other ways to stay safe in the sun? Tell your partner.

Day 5

Weekly Question

Why do we need the sun?

1. Complete each sentence. Fill in the bubble next to the correct answer.

The sun gives us _____.

Ⓐ water   Ⓑ energy   Ⓒ cold air

Plants need the sun to _____.

Ⓐ grow   Ⓑ see   Ⓒ play

Plants and animals need _____ to live.

Ⓐ light and heat   Ⓑ toys and books

2. Complete the sentences.
Use the words in the box.

Earth   sun   heat

Animals need light and _____ from the sun.

Plants need light from the _____ to make food.

There would be no life on _____ without the sun.

Day 1

Daily Science

Big Idea 3

WEEK 4

The **moon** is close to Earth. It is much closer to Earth than the sun is. But the moon is not like Earth. It is much smaller. It does not have air or water.

Vocabulary

moon
a large object near Earth that is made from rock and gets light from the sun

1. Color the picture. Circle the sun.
   Draw a box around the moon.

2. Complete the sentences. Circle the correct words.

   The moon is _____ Earth than the sun is.

   closer to   farther from

   Earth is _____ than the moon.

   bigger   smaller

   There is no water or air on _____.

   Earth   the moon

Day 2

Daily Science

Big Idea 3

WEEK 4

The moon is made of rock. It has **mountains** and **craters**. The craters look like bowls. They were made by things that crashed into the moon.

Vocabulary

crater
a hole on the surface of the moon that is shaped like a bowl

mountain
a very tall object made from dirt and rocks

1. Look at the picture of the moon. Write the words.

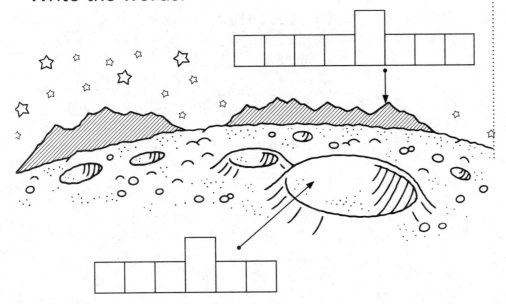

2. Complete the sentences. Use the words in the box.

crater   rock

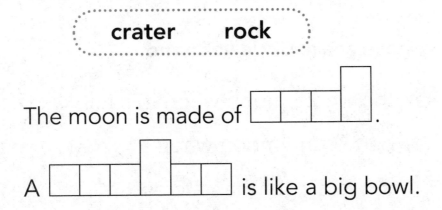

The moon is made of ⬚⬚⬚⬚.

A ⬚⬚⬚⬚⬚⬚ is like a big bowl.

Can anything live on the moon?

The moon gets light from the sun. But we can't always see the side of the moon that is in the sunlight. That is why the moon looks like it changes shape.

1. Color the picture. Use yellow for the part of the moon that is lit up. Use black for the part that is dark.

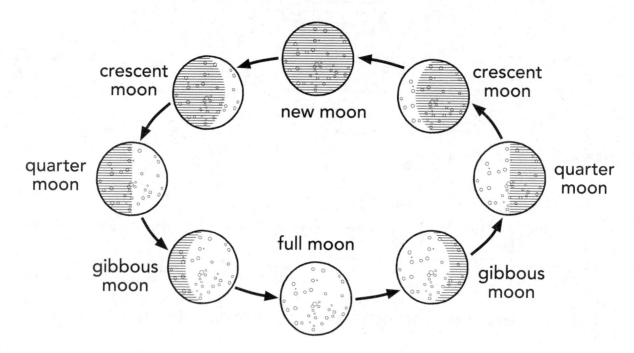

2. Look at the picture again. Circle yes or no.

You can see the whole moon when it is full.   yes   no

You can see part of the moon when it is new.   yes   no

A quarter moon is bigger than a crescent.   yes   no

Day 4

Weekly Question

Can anything live on the moon?

The moon is so close that we can visit it. We went to the moon in 1969. But we had to take our own air and water. Without air and water, we could not visit the moon.

1. Complete the rhymes. Use the words in the box.

> air   moon   water

Someday soon,

You might go to the _____.

If you do go there,

Be sure to take some _____!

The trip is longer than you think,

So take _____ to drink.

2. Color the picture.

Day 5

Can anything live on the moon?

1. Read the sentences. Circle **yes** or **no**.

The moon is made of rock.	yes	no
The moon has air and water.	yes	no
The moon has craters.	yes	no
The moon makes its own light.	yes	no

2. Name each picture. Write the words from the box.

> full   new   crescent

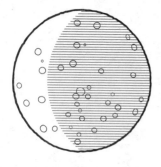 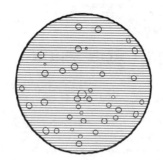 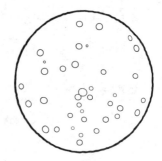

_____   _____   _____

3. Answer the question. Write **yes** or **no**.

Can anything live on the moon? _____

Looking at the Sky

Read each sentence. Fill in the bubble next to the correct answer.

1. When can we see stars, planets, and the moon?

Ⓐ mostly during the day

Ⓑ mostly at night

Ⓒ all the time

2. We have day and night because _____.

Ⓐ the sun spins

Ⓑ the sun moves across the sky

Ⓒ Earth rotates

3. The sun's energy gives Earth _____.

Ⓐ light and heat

Ⓑ a moon and stars

Ⓒ rocks and water

4. The moon does <u>not</u> have _____.

Ⓐ craters

Ⓑ air and water

Ⓒ rocks

Unit Review

Vocabulary

Be a Word Star!

Daily Science

Big Idea 3

WEEK 5

1. Circle the word that completes each sentence.

Earth and Mars are both _____.

planets   stars   moons

The moon has mountains and _____.

energy   planets   craters

Earth _____ once every day.

heats   lights   rotates

2. Match each word on the left to its meaning.

heat •   • the object that is closest to Earth

night •   • the time after the sun rises

moon •   • energy we can see

light •   • energy we can feel

day •   • the time after the sun sets

Unit Review

Visual Literacy
Night and Day

Daily Science
Big
Idea 3

WEEK 5

Look at each picture. Read the captions below it. Fill in the bubble next to the caption that tells about the picture.

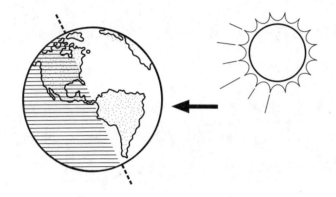

1. Ⓐ It is day here.

   Ⓑ We see stars at night.

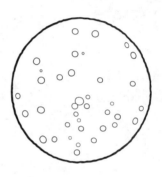

2. Ⓐ It is day.

   Ⓑ The moon is full.

3. Ⓐ The moon gives us light.

   Ⓑ The sun gives us light.

4. Ⓐ Earth rotates.

   Ⓑ We need the sun to live.

Moon Phase Fun

See how the moon looks to us as it goes around Earth.

What You Need

- a paper plate
- yellow and black markers or crayons

1. Get a number from your teacher.

2. Make your plate look like the moon that matches your number. Color your plate and add craters.

3. Stand in the right spot for your moon phase. Hold the plate high above your head!

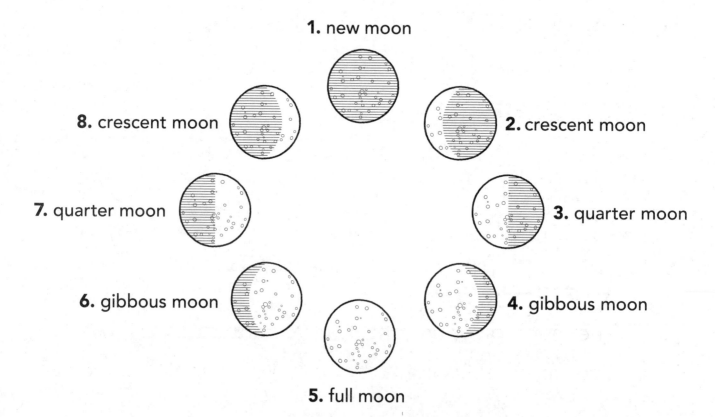

1. new moon

8. crescent moon

2. crescent moon

7. quarter moon

3. quarter moon

6. gibbous moon

4. gibbous moon

5. full moon

Which moon did you make? Write its name. _____

Day 1

Weekly Question

Why is it hot in the summer?

Daily Science

Big Idea 4

WEEK 1

There are four **seasons** during the year. **Summer** is the season between spring and fall. It is hot during the summer. The days are long. Plants grow during the summer. Many people like to be outside.

Vocabulary

season
a time of year with its own weather

summer
the season with the warmest weather

1. Complete the sentences. Write the words.

Each year has four ☐☐☐☐☐☐☐ .

The days in ☐☐☐☐☐☐ are long.

Plants grow the most during ☐☐☐☐☐☐ .

2. Circle what people do in the summer.

© Evan-Moor Corp. • EMC 6871 • Daily Science

73

Imagine a line that runs through the middle of Earth, from top to bottom. The line is tilted. This is Earth's **axis**. It is not a real line. It just helps us understand how Earth spins.

Vocabulary

axis
an imaginary line that runs from Earth's north pole to its south pole

1. Look at the picture. Write the word. Then color Earth.

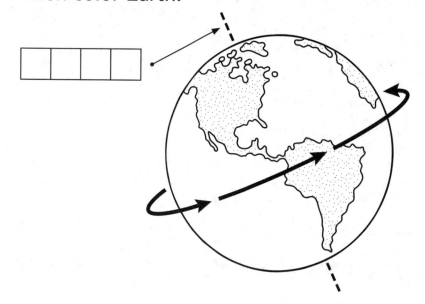

2. Read each sentence. Circle **yes** or **no**.

Earth's axis is a real line.   yes   no

Earth's axis ends in the middle of the planet.   yes   no

Earth's axis is tilted.   yes   no

Weekly Question
Why is it hot in the summer?

Earth **orbits**, or moves around, the sun. As it does, the part of Earth that is tilted toward the sun gets more sunshine. That is when it is summer.

Vocabulary

orbit
to move in a circle around something. Earth orbits the sun.

1. Trace Earth's orbit. Circle the house where it is summer.

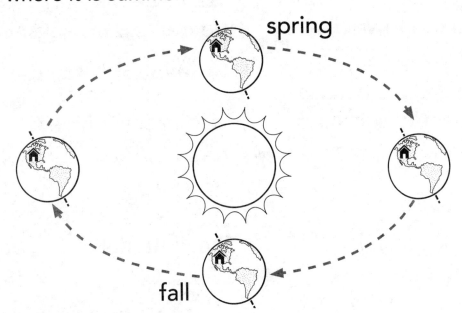

spring

fall

2. Complete the sentences. Write the words.

Earth ☐☐☐☐☐ around the sun.

Earth gets a lot of sun in the summer because

its ☐☐☐ is tilted toward the sun.

Daily Science

Big
Idea 4

WEEK 1

Day 4

Weekly Question

Why is it hot in the summer?

The extra sunshine we get in summer makes the weather hot. It makes the days longer, too.

1. Look at the chart. Read each cause. Circle the effect.

Cause		Effect
Earth is tilted toward the sun in summer.	→	We get _____ sunshine. a lot of a little
We get a lot of sunshine during summer.	→	The sunshine makes the weather _____. cool hot
We get a lot of light during summer.	→	The light makes the days _____. short long

2. Complete the sentences. Write the words.

We get more light and heat in ☐☐☐☐☐☐ .

This is because we get more ☐☐☐ in summer.

76   Daily Science • EMC 6871 • © Evan-Moor Corp.

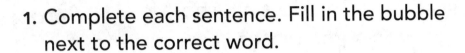

Day 5

Weekly Question

Why is it hot in the summer?

WEEK 1

1. Complete each sentence. Fill in the bubble next to the correct word.

Earth's _____ runs from the top to the bottom.

Ⓐ tilt   Ⓑ axis   Ⓒ summer

The season with the warmest weather is _____.

Ⓐ fall   Ⓑ spring   Ⓒ summer

As Earth moves around the sun, we get _____.

Ⓐ axis   Ⓑ seasons   Ⓒ tilt

Earth _____ the sun once every year.

Ⓐ orbits   Ⓑ visits   Ⓒ passes

2. Look at the picture. Write the words from the box.

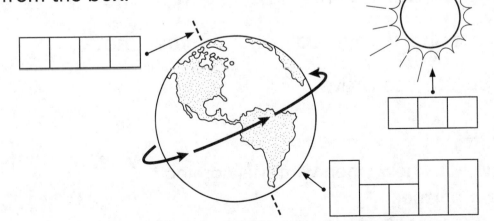

axis

Earth

sun

Why does it snow in the winter?

Winter is the coldest season. The days are shorter. Many plants do not grow. In some places, it snows.

1. Complete each sentence. Write the word.

Some places have a very cold

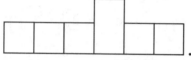
.

Plants do not grow during

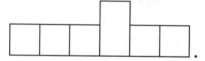
.

Vocabulary

winter
the coldest season, between fall and spring

2. Read the sentences. Do these things happen where you live during winter? Circle **yes** or **no**.

People swim outside.	yes	no
People wear coats and hats.	yes	no
Days are shorter and colder.	yes	no
Flowers start to grow.	yes	no

 Talk

How do you know when winter is coming? Tell your partner.

Day 2

Weekly Question

Why does it snow in the winter?

Our part of Earth is tilted away from the sun during winter. We get less sunlight. The **temperature** goes down.

Vocabulary

temperature
how hot or cold something is

1. Where is it winter? Put an **X** in the correct box. Then complete the sentence.

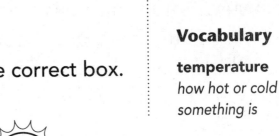

Less sunlight means a lower

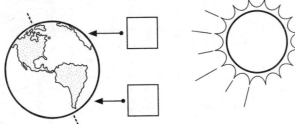

.

2. Do you think the temperature in each place is **warm** or **cold**? Circle your answer.

warm   cold

warm   cold

warm   cold

Why does it snow in the winter?

We use a **thermometer** to tell us how hot or cold something is. A thermometer measures temperature in degrees. During winter, the temperature in some places goes below 32 degrees. That's cold enough to freeze water!

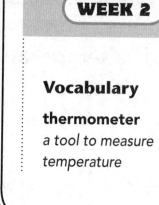

32° ➡

Vocabulary

thermometer
a tool to measure temperature

1. Write the word.

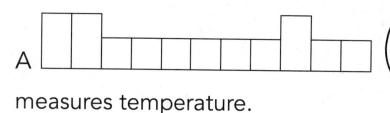

A ⬚⬚ ⬚⬚⬚⬚⬚⬚ ⬚⬚

measures temperature.

2. Write the number. Color up to it on the thermometer.

When the temperature is _____ degrees, water freezes.

3. Read each thermometer. Write the temperature.

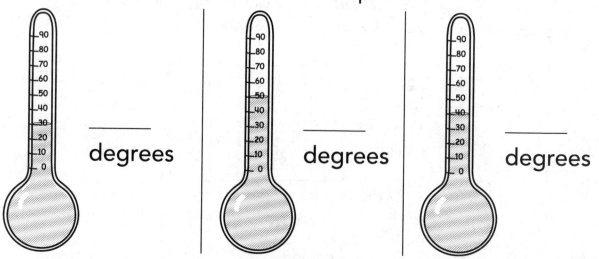

_____ degrees   _____ degrees   _____ degrees

Day 4

Weekly Question

Why does it snow in the winter?

In places where the temperature goes below 32 degrees, **snow** may fall. Snow is made of tiny frozen drops of water. They are called **snowflakes**. **Icicles** may also form in the winter.

Vocabulary

icicles
long, thin pieces of ice made from dripping water that has frozen

snow
tiny frozen drops of water, stuck together

snowflakes
tiny frozen drops of water

1. Match the pictures on the left to the big picture.

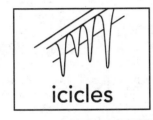

icicles

snowflakes

2. Complete the sentence. Write the word.

   It may ☐☐☐☐ in the winter.

3. Read each sentence. Circle **yes** or **no**.

   Snow is made from icicles.   yes   no

   Snow can form when it is
   colder than 32 degrees.   yes   no

   Snowflakes and icicles are
   made from frozen water.   yes   no

© Evan-Moor Corp. • EMC 6871 • *Daily Science*   81

Day 5

Weekly Question

Why does it snow in the winter?

Daily Science
Big Idea 4
WEEK 2

1. Complete each sentence. Circle the correct answer.

The coldest season of the year is _____.

summer   fall   winter

The _____ is how hot or cold something is.

winter   temperature   weather

A _____ is a tool that measures temperature.

snowflake   thermometer   ruler

In winter, our part of Earth is tilted _____ the sun.

away from   toward   around

2. Look at each thermometer. Does it show
   above or **below** freezing? Write the word.

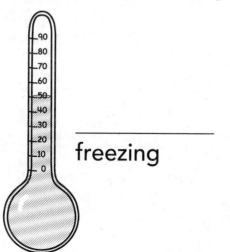 _____ freezing

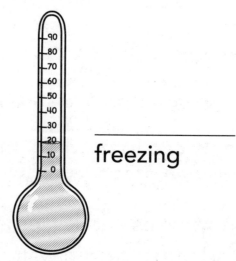 _____ freezing

Day 1

Weekly Question
Why are there a lot of flowers in the spring?

Spring is the season between winter and summer. The temperature gets warmer. The days get longer.

1. Trace Earth's orbit. Circle the house where it is spring.

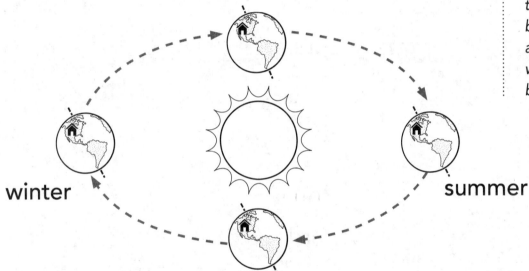

winter

summer

Vocabulary

spring
the season between winter and summer, when the weather becomes warmer

2. Complete the sentence. Write the word.

In [⬚⬚⬚⬚] , the weather gets warmer.

3. Read each question. Circle the answer.

What season comes after spring?   summer   winter

What season has longer days?   winter   spring

Day 2

Why are there a lot of flowers in the spring?

Daily Science

Big Idea 4

WEEK 3

Plants need heat and light to grow. When spring comes, plants get more heat and light. **Flowers** begin to **bloom**.

Color the picture below.
Then complete the sentences.

Vocabulary

bloom
to grow and open

flowers
the parts of plants that make seeds and fruit

In spring, many plants grow ⬜⬜ ⬜⬜⬜⬜ .

The flowers start to ⬜⬜ ⬜⬜ .

 Talk

What do you think would happen to plants if spring was cold like winter? Tell your partner.

Day 3

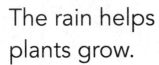

Weekly Question

Why are there a lot of flowers in the spring?

Daily Science

Big Idea 4

WEEK 3

Some places get a lot of **rain** in spring. Warm, wet air mixes with cold air. The two kinds of air make rain clouds. The rain helps plants grow.

Vocabulary

rain
water drops that fall from clouds

1. Read each sentence. Draw a line to the matching picture.

The rain helps plants grow.   •

•

Warm air and cold air make rain clouds.   •

•

Plants make new flowers in spring.   •

•

2. Complete the poem. Draw a picture of yourself in the rain.

The sun is gone.

The ☐☐☐☐ has begun.

I'm getting wet,

But I'm having fun!

Weekly Question

Why are there a lot of flowers in the spring?

There are many kinds of flowers in spring. Some are big. Some have a lot of colors. Some flowers smell sweet. But they all need the same things. They need warmth, light, and water. That is why they all bloom in the spring!

1. Read the name of each flower.
   Then color the pictures.

rose

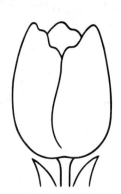

tulip

daffodil

2. Read each sentence. Circle **yes** or **no**.

Flowers need light and water to grow.   yes   no

All flowers smell bad.   yes   no

There are many kinds of flowers.   yes   no

Day 5

Weekly Question

Why are there a lot of flowers in the spring?

1. Read the sentences. Do these things happen in the spring? Circle **yes** or **no**.

There is a lot of rain in some places.	yes	no
The days are shorter and colder.	yes	no
Plants grow and make flowers.	yes	no

2. Complete the sentence. Write the word.

   The season after winter is 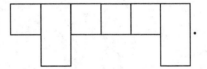 .

3. Look at the pictures.
   What happens first? Write **1** under it.
   What happens next? Write **2** under it.
   What happens last? Write **3** under it.

_____   _____   _____

Day 1

Weekly Question

Why do some trees lose their leaves in the fall?

Daily Science

Big Idea 4

WEEK 4

Fall is the season after summer and before winter. Another name for fall is **autumn**. The weather gets colder. The days get shorter. Leaves on some trees turn red, orange, yellow, and brown. Then the leaves fall off.

Vocabulary

autumn or **fall**
the season between summer and winter, when there is less daylight and the weather cools

1. Color the leaves. Then complete the sentence.

In the ☐☐☐ , leaves turn many colors.

2. Which of these happens in the fall? Circle the picture.

Daily Science • EMC 6871 • © Evan-Moor Corp.

Day 2

Weekly Question

Why do some trees lose their leaves in the fall?

In the fall, Earth begins to tilt away from the sun. Less sunlight means the days start growing shorter. The weather begins to cool. Winter is coming. Plants must get ready.

1. Circle the house where it is fall.

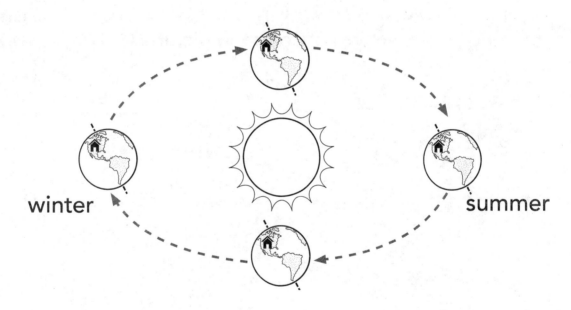

winter   summer

2. Read each cause. Draw a line to its effect.

Cause			Effect
Earth gets less sunlight in the fall.	•	•	We have four seasons.
Earth orbits the sun.	•	•	Days are cooler and shorter.

Weekly Question

Why do some trees lose their leaves in the fall?

In the fall, the warm and wet air of summer is replaced by cool and dry air. When warm and cool air mix, they make **wind**. The wind helps blow leaves off the trees. A **gust** is a big wind. A **breeze** is a small wind.

Vocabulary

wind
air that is moving

breeze
a light wind

gust
a strong wind

1. Look at the picture. Which way is the wind blowing? Draw an arrow. Color the picture.

2. Complete the poem. Use the words in the box.

> breeze   gust

A little _____ is nice and soft.

But a strong _____ blows your hat right off!

Day 4

Weekly Question

Why do some trees lose their leaves in the fall?

Trees use their leaves to get energy from the sun. But in the fall, there is less sunlight because the days are shorter. The cold, dry air makes leaves dry up and fall off.

1. Complete the sentences. Circle the correct words.

   There is _____ sunlight in the fall.

   more   less

   Air that is _____ makes leaves fall off trees.

   cold and dry   warm and wet

2. Draw a tree in the fall. Show the wind blowing the leaves. Color the leaves different colors.

Day 5

Weekly Question

Why do some trees lose their leaves in the fall?

Daily Science

Big Idea 4

WEEK 4

1. Read each question. Fill in the bubble next to the correct word.

What season comes right after summer?

Ⓐ spring   Ⓑ winter   Ⓒ autumn

What is the name for a small wind?

Ⓐ gust   Ⓑ breeze   Ⓒ fall

What do you get when cool and warm air mix?

Ⓐ leaves   Ⓑ sunlight   Ⓒ wind

2. Read each sentence. Put a check mark in front of the sentences that tell why trees lose their leaves in the fall.

___ The weather gets cooler.

___ Animals eat all the leaves.

___ The wind blows leaves off trees.

___ People take the leaves because they are pretty.

___ There is less sunlight for leaves.

Comprehension

Seasons and Weather

Read each question. Fill in the bubble next to the correct answer.

1. Which season is the hottest?

Ⓒ winter

Ⓓ spring

Ⓔ summer

Ⓕ fall

2. Which season is the coldest?

Ⓒ winter

Ⓓ spring

Ⓔ summer

Ⓕ fall

3. When do trees drop their leaves?

Ⓒ winter

Ⓓ spring

Ⓔ summer

Ⓕ fall

4. Which season has the most new flowers?

Ⓒ winter

Ⓓ spring

Ⓔ summer

Ⓕ fall

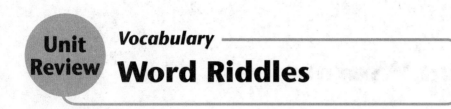

Unit Review

Vocabulary

Word Riddles

Daily Science

Big Idea 4

WEEK 5

Read each riddle. Circle the correct answer.

1. I am a season that brings warm weather, rain, and flowers.

    spring   breeze   bloom   fall

2. I am a tool that helps you know how hot it is.

    summer   thermometer   flower   gust

3. I am the coldest season, and sometimes I bring snow.

    wind   winter   temperature   rain

4. I am the line that runs from Earth's top to bottom.

    icicle   season   axis   orbit

5. I am the season that happens when Earth tilts toward the sun.

    winter   summer   autumn   spring

Unit Review

Visual Literacy

The Changing Seasons

Look at the chart. Write the name of each season in the correct order. Then draw how a tree looks during that season.

> winter   spring   summer   fall

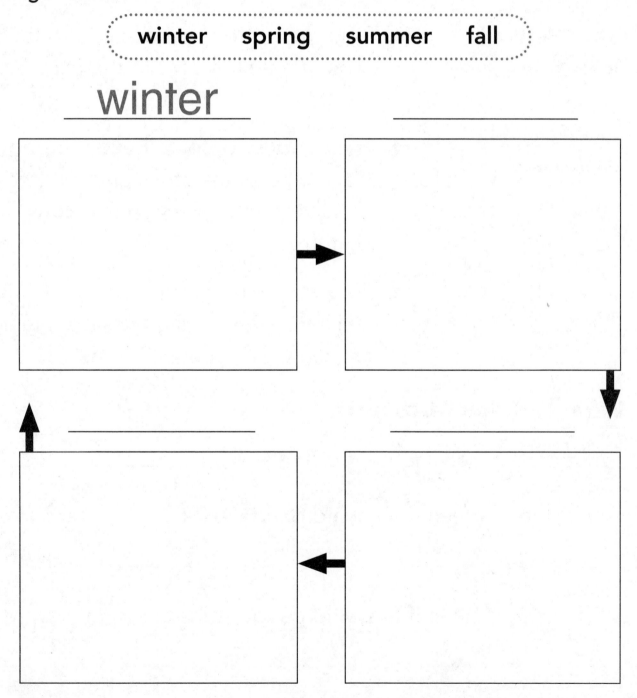

winter

_____

_____

_____

Measure the Wind!

You cannot see the wind. But you can see it move things. Make a wind gauge. See if the wind is moving fast, slow, or not at all.

What You Need

- unsharpened pencil
- 2 small paper cups
- drinking straw
- pin and tape

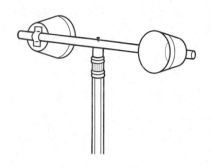

1. Tape the bottom of each cup to the ends of the straw. Make the cups face in different directions.

2. Ask an adult to poke the pin through the middle of the straw and into the pencil eraser. Make sure the straw will turn.

3. Hold your wind gauge outside. Check at different times of day. Is it spinning fast, slow, or not at all?

What Did You Discover?

What makes the wind gauge spin? _____

What does it mean if the wind gauge is still?

_____

What does it mean if the wind gauge spins fast?

_____

Day 1

Weekly Question

Why can't we walk through walls?

Everything in the world is made of **matter**.
A **solid** is a kind of matter that keeps its shape.
A wall is a solid.
So is a person.

Vocabulary

matter
everything that takes up space

solid
matter that keeps its shape and size

1. Complete the sentences. Write the words.

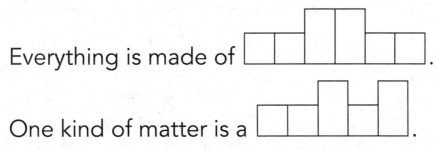

Everything is made of ⬚⬚⬚⬚⬚ .

One kind of matter is a ⬚⬚⬚⬚ .

2. Complete the sentences. Use the words in the box.

A _____ is a solid.

A _____ is a solid.

A _____ is a solid.

ball

block

pen

Mass is how much matter something is made of. You can measure the mass of a solid. You can also describe the **shape** of a solid.

Vocabulary

mass
the amount of matter something has

shape
the form or outline of an object

1. Complete each sentence. Write the word.

   A book has more ☐☐☐☐ than a pencil.

   A cat has more ☐☐☐ than a mouse.

2. Trace each shape. Draw a line to the solid it matches.

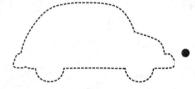

3. Complete the sentence. Write the word.

   Every solid has a 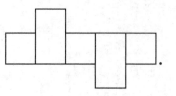 .

Day 3

Weekly Question
Why can't we walk through walls?

You can mix solids together. This makes a **mixture**. The solids in a mixture do not change shape. They just get mixed up. They can still be sorted out of the mixture.

Vocabulary

mixture
solids mixed together

1. Complete the sentence. Write the word.

A ⬚⬚⬚⬚⬚⬚ is made of solids that are mixed together.

2. Look at the mixture of toys on the left. Circle the things on the right that are part of the mixture.

Day 4

Weekly Question
Why can't we walk through walls?

Daily Science

Big Idea 5

WEEK 1

A person and a wall are both solid. A solid can't change its shape. If you tried to walk through a wall, you would hurt yourself!

1. Complete the rhyme. Write the words from the box.

> **wall   nose**

You can walk through a hall,

but not through a _____.

You would stub your toes

and bump your _____!

2. Read each sentence. Circle yes or no.

You can walk through an open door.   yes   no

You can walk through a closed door.   yes   no

Daily Science • EMC 6871 • © Evan-Moor Corp.

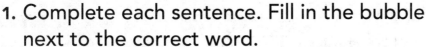

Day 5

Weekly Question

Why can't we walk through walls?

Daily Science

Big Idea 5

WEEK 1

1. Complete each sentence. Fill in the bubble next to the correct word.

A brick is a _____.

Ⓐ wall   Ⓑ solid   Ⓒ matter

Everything is made of _____.

Ⓐ solids   Ⓑ mixtures   Ⓒ matter

An elephant has more _____ than a puppy.

Ⓐ mass   Ⓑ shape   Ⓒ solid

Because a solid keeps its _____,
a person cannot walk through a wall.

Ⓐ mixture   Ⓑ shape   Ⓒ mass

2. Draw a solid in your classroom. Write its name.

_____
(name of solid)

Day 1

Why does water splash?

Daily Science

Big Idea 5

WEEK 2

Water is a **liquid**. A liquid is a kind of matter. When you pour a liquid, it **flows**.

1. Complete each sentence. Write the word.

Matter that flows is called a

[ ] [ ] [ ] [ ] [ ] [ ] .

Water is a kind of [ ] [ ] [ ] [ ] [ ] [ ] .

You can pour a [ ] [ ] [ ] [ ] [ ] [ ] .

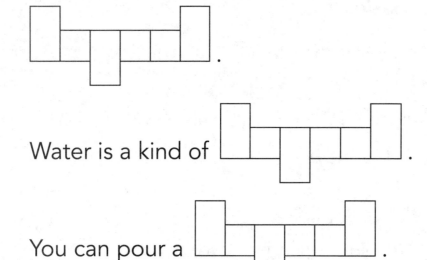

Vocabulary

flows
moves or spreads

liquid
matter that flows and takes the shape of its container

2. Look at the pictures. Circle the things that show liquids.

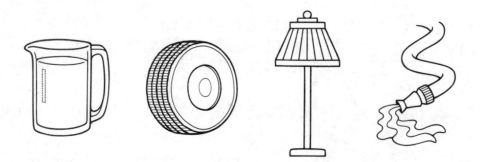

Day 2

Weekly Question

Why does water splash?

A liquid has **mass**, but it does not have a shape. It forms the shape of the container it is in. If you pour water into a cup, the water becomes the shape of the cup.

Vocabulary

mass
the amount of matter something has

Look at each container. Draw a line to the shape of the liquid that is inside it.

 Talk!

How are a solid and a liquid the same?
How are they different? Tell your partner.

Day 3

Weekly Question
Why does water splash?

Daily Science
Big Idea 5

WEEK 2

When a liquid spills, it spreads out. It flows in different directions. It does not stop until it hits something.

1. Mop up as much water as you can!
Draw a line from the mop to the pail.

2. Read each sentence. Circle **yes** or **no**.

A liquid spreads out when it spills.   yes   no

A liquid flows in only one direction.   yes   no

A liquid stops moving when it hits something.   yes   no

Day 4

Weekly Question

Why does water splash?

WEEK 2

When you drop a ball, it bounces. When you drop a book, it lands with a thud. That's because solids keep their shape. But when you drop a liquid, it **splashes**, or spreads apart.

Vocabulary

splash
to spread apart suddenly

1. **Look at the objects. Imagine that they all hit the ground. Cross out the ones that keep their shape. Circle the ones that splash.**

2. **Tell about each picture. Write a word from the box.**

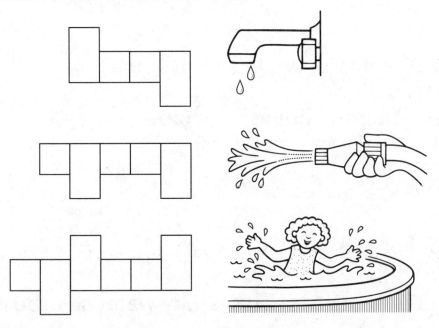

splash

drip

spray

Day 5

Weekly Question

Why does water splash?

1. Complete each sentence. Circle the correct word.

You can pour a _____.

    solid   mass   liquid

Liquids do <u>not</u> have their own _____.

    color   shape   solid

Liquids and solids are both _____.

    matter   water   shapes

Liquid in a cup will be shaped like a _____.

    bowl   cup   spill

2. Complete each sentence. Use the words in the box.

> flow   liquid   shape

Water is a _____.

It does not keep its _____.

It likes to _____. This is why water splashes!

Daily Science • EMC 6871 • © Evan-Moor Corp.

Why do balloons float in the air?

Balloons have air in them. Air is a **gas**. A gas is a kind of matter. It has mass and takes up space. You can't see air. But you can feel it when it moves.

Vocabulary

gas
matter that has little mass and takes the shape of its container

1. Look at the picture. Trace the words.

liquid

solid

gas

2. Complete each sentence. Circle the word.

Air is a _____.   solid   liquid   gas

You can't see _____.   air   liquid   matter

A gas has _____.   liquid   mass   balloons

Day 2

Weekly Question
Why do balloons float in the air?

Daily Science
Big Idea 5

WEEK 3

A gas has no shape. It takes the shape of the container it is in. When you blow up a balloon, you are filling it with air. The air forms the shape of the balloon.

air

1. Match each object on the left to the picture that shows it filled with air.

   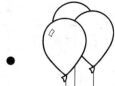

2. Complete the sentences. Write the words from the box.

> fills   air

Andi's bike has a flat tire. It needs _____.

Andi _____ the tire with air.

Day 3

Why do balloons float in the air?

A gas has less **mass** than a liquid or solid. So, things full of gas have less mass than things full of liquids or solids.

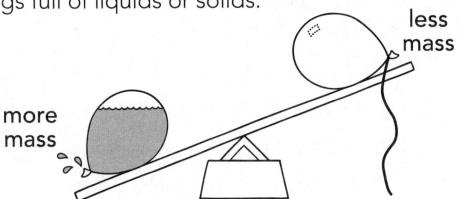

less mass

more mass

Vocabulary

mass
the amount of matter something has

1. Complete each sentence. Write the word.

   A gas has less ☐☐☐☐ than a liquid.

   A balloon full of air has less ☐☐☐☐ than a balloon full of water.

2. Look at each pair. Circle the object with **less** mass.

water   air   air   sand   air   pennies

Weekly Question

Day 4

Why do balloons float in the air?

Daily Science

Big Idea 5

WEEK 3

Not all gases have the same mass. One kind of gas is called **helium**. It has less mass than air. Some balloons have helium in them. They are lighter than air. These balloons will float away if you don't hold on to them!

1. Circle the balloons that have helium in them. Color the picture.

2. Complete each sentence. Use the words in the box.

> **gas   mass**

Helium is a ⬚⬚. Air is a ⬚⬚, too.

Helium and air both have ⬚⬚⬚.

But helium has less ⬚⬚⬚⬚ than air does.

Why do balloons float in the air?

1. Read each sentence. Circle **yes** or **no**.

   Air is a kind of matter.   yes   no

   A gas has its own shape.   yes   no

   A gas has more mass than a liquid.   yes   no

2. Complete each sentence. Use the words in the box.

   > float   gas   mass

   The air we breathe is a _____.

   Some gases have less _____ than air does.

   A balloon filled with these gases will _____.

3. Draw a picture.
   Put balloons in it.

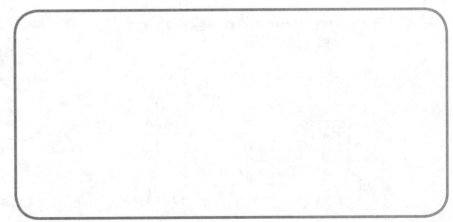

Day 1

Weekly Question
Why does ice melt?

When water freezes, it turns into **ice**. It becomes a **solid**. It keeps its shape. Ice can be thick, like an iceberg. It can be tiny, like a snowflake.

1. **What does ice look like? How does it feel? Trace the words that tell about ice.**

cold   hard

clear   slippery

2. **Complete the sentence. Write the word.**

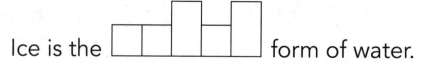

Ice is the ⬚⬚⬚⬚ form of water.

3. **Circle the things made of ice.**

Vocabulary

ice
frozen water

solid
matter that keeps its shape and size

Day 2

Weekly Question

Why does ice melt?

Daily Science

Big Idea 5

WEEK 4

When ice warms up, something happens. It **melts**. It turns into a **liquid**, and it loses its shape.

1. Look at the picture. Then write the words.

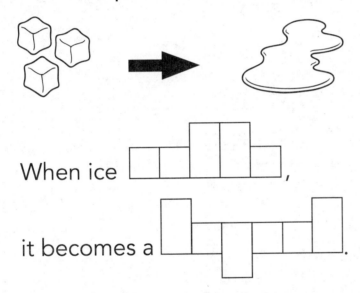

When ice ⬚⬚⬚ ,

it becomes a ⬚⬚⬚ .

Vocabulary

liquid
matter that flows and takes the shape of its container

melts
changes from a solid to a liquid by heating

2. Look at the pictures. Match each picture to what happens after the ice melts.

© Evan-Moor Corp. • EMC 6871 • *Daily Science*

113

Day 3

Weekly Question

Why does ice melt?

 **Daily Science**

Big Idea 5

WEEK 4

Heat makes ice melt. Heat makes some other solids turn into liquids, too.

1. Look at each object on the left. What would it look like if it melted? Match the pictures.

 •

 •

 •

Vocabulary

heat
a form of energy we can feel

2. Answer the riddle. Write the word.

I can turn ice cream into soup.

I can make a tall candle short.

I can turn butter into a puddle.

What am I?

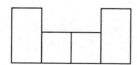

114

Daily Science • EMC 6871 • © Evan-Moor Corp.

Weekly Question

Why does ice melt?

Ice is the solid form of water. The gas form of water is **steam**. When water gets very hot, it boils. The heat turns the water into steam. You can see the steam rising from a pot of boiling water.

Vocabulary

steam
the gas form of water

1. Color the fire red. Draw the steam coming out of the kettle. Then write its name.

_____

2. Read each sentence. Circle **yes** or **no**.

The solid form of water is steam.	yes	no
Heat turns water into steam.	yes	no
You can see steam.	yes	no

Day 5

Weekly Question

Why does ice melt?

Daily Science

Big Idea 5

WEEK 4

1. Draw a line to match each form of water to the type of matter it is.

    water •   • solid

    steam •   • liquid

    ice •   • gas

2. Answer the questions. Write the words.

   What makes ice melt?   _____

   What turns water into steam? _____

   What form of matter is steam? _____

3. Look at the pictures below. Draw what happens to them when they get hot.

Daily Science • EMC 6871 • © Evan-Moor Corp.

Solids, Liquids, and Gases

Read each sentence. Fill in the bubble next to the correct answer.

1. What does a solid do?

   Ⓐ It keeps its shape.

   Ⓑ It flows.

   Ⓒ It fills a container.

2. Heat turns liquid water into a _____.

   Ⓐ solid

   Ⓑ liquid

   Ⓒ gas

3. Which of these have mass?

   Ⓐ liquid   Ⓒ gas

   Ⓑ solid   Ⓓ all of these

4. What do you get when you mix solids?

   Ⓐ a liquid   Ⓒ a gas

   Ⓑ a mixture   Ⓓ steam

Draw lines to match the words to their meanings.

mixture •   • frozen water

liquid •   • energy we can feel

matter •   • everything that takes up space

ice •   • the gas form of water

steam •   • matter that flows

heat •   • a mix of solids

gas •   • matter that keeps its shape and size

mass •   • the amount of matter something has

solid •   • to change a solid to a liquid by heating

shape •   • to spread apart suddenly

melt •   • the form or outline of an object

splash •   • matter that has little mass and takes the shape of its container

Visual Literacy

What Do You See?

Look at each picture. Is it a **solid**, **liquid**, or **gas**? Circle the correct word.

solid   liquid   gas

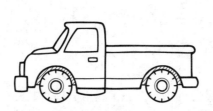

solid   liquid   gas

solid   liquid   gas

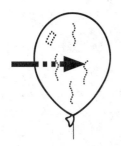

solid   liquid   gas

solid   liquid   gas

solid   liquid   gas

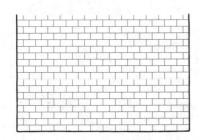

solid   liquid   gas

solid   liquid   gas

solid   liquid   gas

© Evan-Moor Corp. • EMC 6871 • *Daily Science*

Ice Cube Race

What You Need

- ice cube trays
- plastic cups
- marbles

1. Have your teacher freeze a marble in each square of water in an ice cube tray.

2. Take an ice cube out of the tray. Put it in a cup.

3. Now try to melt the ice cube and free the marble. But you can't touch the marble or the ice cube!

4. Watch the clock to see how long it takes to free the marble. Race with a partner!

What Did You Discover?

How long did it take you to free the marble?

_____

Who won the race? _____

What did you do to make the ice cube melt?

_____

_____

Day 1

Why do shopping carts have wheels?

Daily Science

Big Idea 6

WEEK 1

As soon as you got out of bed today, you used **motion**. That means you moved. All kinds of things use motion.

Vocabulary

motion
moving from one place to another

1. Look at the picture. Circle the things in motion.

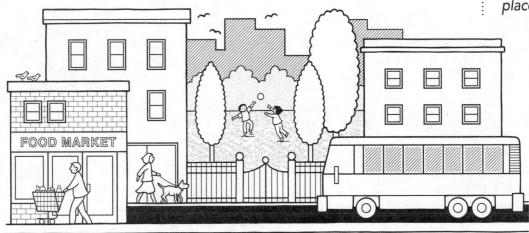

FOOD MARKET

2. Complete each sentence. Write the word.

A car uses ☐☐☐☐☐ to go down the road.

A person uses ☐☐☐☐☐ to walk up stairs.

 Talk

Think of some things you did today that used motion. Tell your partner.

Day 2

Weekly Question

Why do shopping carts have wheels?

It takes **force** to move something. A force can be a **push** or a **pull**. You can push or pull a shopping cart.

Vocabulary

force
something that makes an object move

pull
to bring an object closer

push
to move an object farther away

1. Complete each sentence. Use the words in the box.

pull

push

You 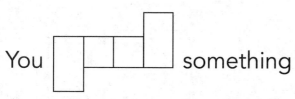 something

to move it away from you.

You 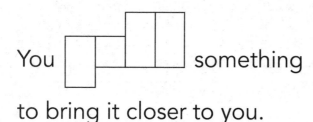 something

to bring it closer to you.

2. Look at each picture. Is it a **push** or a **pull**? Write the word below the picture.

_____ _____ _____

Day 3

Why do shopping carts have wheels?

Daily Science

Big Idea 6

WEEK 1

Imagine trying to move a shopping cart without wheels! A **wheel** makes it easier to push or pull something. You use less force to move something that has wheels.

Vocabulary

wheel
a round object that rolls or turns

1. Answer the riddle. Write the word.

I spin and spin.

I'm round like a pie.

Just try to stop me

When I roll by.

What am I?

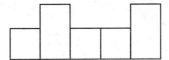

2. What are some things that have wheels?
   Draw a picture of something that has wheels.
   Then write its name.

123

Day 4

Weekly Question

Why do shopping carts have wheels?

Big, heavy things need a lot of force to move them. Small, light things don't need as much force. A full shopping cart is harder to move than an empty shopping cart.

1. Look at each pair of pictures. Circle the object that needs more force to move.

2. Read each sentence. Circle **yes** or **no**.

A stick is easier to pull than a log.	yes	no
You need a lot of force to push a toy car.	yes	no
You need a little force to pull an empty cart.	yes	no
A marble needs a bigger push than a bowling ball.	yes	no

Day 5

Weekly Question

Why do shopping carts have wheels?

Daily Science

Big Idea 6

WEEK 1

1. Complete each sentence. Circle the correct word.

A push and a pull are kinds of _____.

playing   force   wheels

A ball in _____ moves from one place to another.

force   motion   push

A _____ makes it easier to move heavy things.

wheel   rock   stick

2. Write the name of each picture. Use the words in the box.

> pull   push   wheel

_____   _____   _____

Day 1

Weekly Question

Why does a ball go far when I kick it hard?

Force makes an object move. When an object moves, it goes a certain **distance**. Distance is how far an object moves.

Vocabulary

distance
how far an object moves

1. Look at the picture. Trace the words.

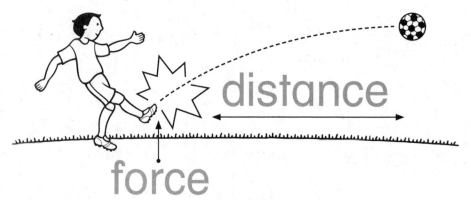

distance

force

2. Look at the picture again. Read the questions. Circle the answers.

What force moved the ball?

the ground   the kick

What distance does the picture show?

how far the ball went   how far the boy ran

What did <u>not</u> move?

the ball   the ground

Day 2

Why does a ball go far when I kick it hard?

If you hit a ball with a lot of force, it will go far. If you hit it with a little force, it will not go as far.

1. The player hits the ball with **a little force**. The ball goes 3 squares. Draw the ball where it lands.

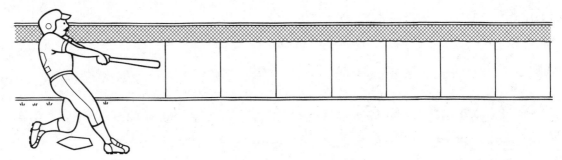

2. The player hits the ball with **a lot of force**. The ball goes 6 squares. Draw the ball where it lands.

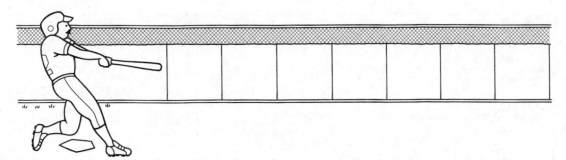

3. Read each sentence. Circle **yes** or **no**.

A ball will move only if you hit it with a big force.　　　yes　　no

A small force will make a ball go farther than a big force.　　　yes　　no

Weekly Question

Day 3

Why does a ball go far when I kick it hard?

How fast or slow something moves is its **speed**. An airplane has a lot of speed. It goes fast. A snail doesn't have much speed. It goes slow.

1. Look at the pictures. Circle the pictures of things that have a lot of speed.

Vocabulary

speed
how fast something moves

2. Look at the graph. Answer the questions.

		slow → fast
bike	🚲	▨▨▨▨▨▨□□
car	🚗	▨▨▨▨▨▨▨▨
turtle	🐢	▨□□□□□□□

Which one has the most speed? _____

Which one is slower than the bike? _____

Day 4

Weekly Question

Why does a ball go far when I kick it hard?

A **kick** is a big force. It will make a ball go far. It will make a ball go fast. A **tap** is a little force. It will not make a ball go as far or as fast.

1. Look at the pictures. Predict what will happen. Put an **X** next to the correct answer.

☐ the ball goes far   ☐ the ball goes a short distance

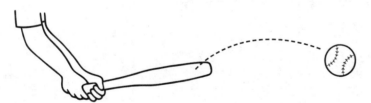

☐ the ball goes far   ☐ the ball goes a short distance

2. Complete the sentences. Write **kick** or **tap**.

I _____ the ball hard to make it go far.

I _____ the ball to move it a little bit.

Weekly Question

Why does a ball go far when I kick it hard?

1. Read each question. Circle the correct answer.

What tells you how fast or slow something is?

speed   force   distance

What tells you how far something goes?

speed   force   distance

What do you use when you kick a ball?

speed   force   distance

2. Look at the graph. Answer the questions.

rocket								
boy								
truck								

slow   fast

Which thing has the most speed? _____

Which thing has the least speed? _____

Day 1

Weekly Question

Why do cars have steering wheels?

When you push or pull something, it moves. That changes where the thing is. You can push or pull something **forward**. You can push or pull something **backward**.

Vocabulary

forward
toward the front

backward
toward the back

1. Look at the picture of the car. Trace the words that tell how the car changes where it is.

forward

backward

2. Read each sentence. Circle **yes** or **no**.

When you pull something, it moves.	yes	no
Force always moves something forward.	yes	no
You can push something backward.	yes	no

Weekly Question
Why do cars have steering wheels?

A **path** shows where something is going. Some paths are straight. Some paths are curved. Some go in a circle.

Vocabulary

path
the distance and direction an object travels

1. Look at the pictures. Draw a line to show the path of each object.

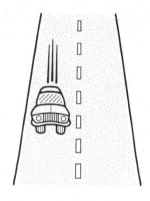

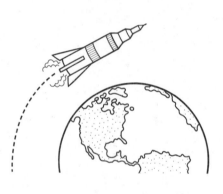

straight   circle   curved

2. Look at the pictures again. Draw a line to the word that completes each sentence.

The train tracks make a _____. •   • straight

The rocket's path is _____. •   • circle

The car is going _____. •   • curved

Day 3

Weekly Question

Why do cars have steering wheels?

You can change the path of an object with **force**. Hitting a ball with a bat changes the ball's path. The bat pushes the ball. The ball moves away from the bat.

Vocabulary

force
something that makes an object move

1. Look at the picture. Trace the path of the ball. Complete the sentences.

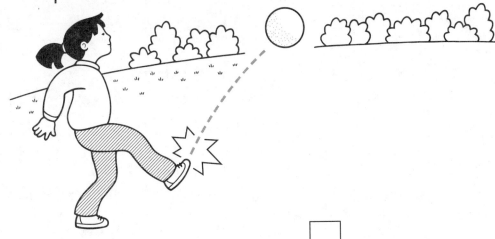

The girl kicks the ball. The ⬚⬚⬚⬚ of the kick

changes the ⬚⬚⬚ of the ball.

2. Read the riddle. Write the answer.

You use me to change an object's path.

I am a kick, a throw, or a hit.

What am I? _____

Day 4

Weekly Question
Why do cars have steering wheels?

A steering wheel changes the path of a car.
When you turn the steering wheel, you use force.
The steering wheel sends that force to the car's
wheels. The wheels move. The car's path changes!

Look at the picture. Help the car get to the lake.
Circle the words to complete the directions.
Then color the picture.

1. To go into the tunnel, _____ the wheel.   turn
                                                       don't turn

2. To get to the lake, _____ the wheel.   turn
                                                       don't turn

3. To go around the lake, _____ the wheel.   turn
                                                       don't turn

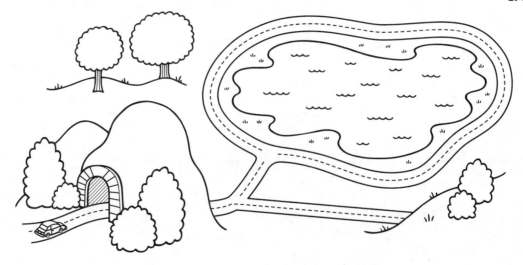

Day 5

Weekly Question
Why do cars have steering wheels?

Daily Science

Big Idea 6

WEEK 3

1. Complete each sentence. Circle the correct word.

All things _____ in a path.

move   stop   circle

A path can be changed by _____.

curve   force   talking

Straight, curved, and in a circle are kinds of _____.

paths   wheels   forces

2. Draw each kind of path.

straight	circle	curved

Day 1

Weekly Question
Why do things fall down when you drop them?

Daily Science

Big Idea 6

WEEK 4

When you throw a ball into the air, it will always come down. This is because a force pulls the ball to the ground. That force is called **gravity**.

1. Look at the picture. Write the word **gravity**.

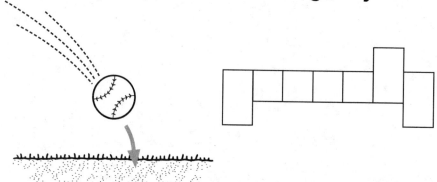

Vocabulary

gravity
a force that pulls things to the ground

2. Complete the poem. Use the words in the box.

fall   force   down   ball

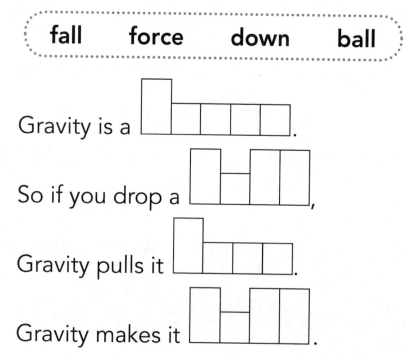

Gravity is a ____.

So if you drop a ____,

Gravity pulls it ____.

Gravity makes it ____.

Daily Science • EMC 6871 • © Evan-Moor Corp.

Daily Science

Big Idea 6

WEEK 4

Gravity pulls things down in a straight line. It pulls on all things the same way. They fall at the same speed. They land at the same time.

1. Draw an arrow to show which way each thing falls.

2. Read each sentence. Circle **yes** or **no**.

Gravity pulls things up.	yes	no
A book and a ball fall at the same speed.	yes	no
A book and a ball land at different times.	yes	no
You use gravity to throw a ball.	yes	no

Day 3

Weekly Question

Why do things fall down when you drop them?

Daily Science

Big Idea 6

WEEK 4

You can use force to keep things from falling. When you lift a cup to drink, you pull the cup to you. Your force keeps the cup up.

1. Look at the pictures. What is holding each thing or person up? Circle it.

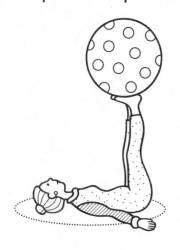

2. Look at the picture. Draw some things for the clown to hold up.

Daily Science • EMC 6871 • © Evan-Moor Corp.

Weekly Question
Why do things fall down when you drop them?

When you get on a slide, you do not fall straight down. You travel the path of the slide. When you push yourself on a swing, you do not fall down. You go back and forth. The slide and the swing change your path. But gravity is still pulling on you.

1. Look at the pictures. Draw the path that each ball will follow as it falls.

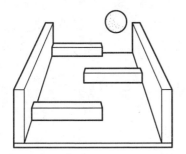 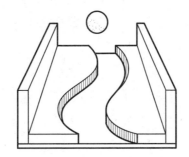 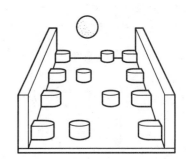

2. Trace the arrows to show how gravity pulls on the swing. Then color the pictures.

Day 5

Weekly Question
Why do things fall down when you drop them?

Daily Science

Big Idea 6

WEEK 4

1. Complete the sentences. Circle the correct words.

The force that pulls everything down is _____.

gravity   a path   the ground

A slide will change the _____ that you follow to the ground.

force   path   gravity

You can use _____ to keep a ball from falling.

gravity   a slide   force

2. Look at the pictures. Draw the path that each ball will follow to the ground.

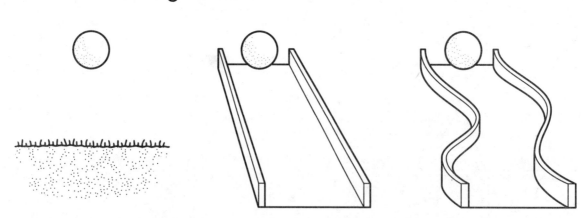

Read each question. Fill in the bubble next to the correct answer.

1. What force makes things fall when you drop them?
   - Ⓐ air
   - Ⓑ gravity
   - Ⓒ speed
   - Ⓓ distance

2. What word describes how far something moves?
   - Ⓐ distance
   - Ⓑ speed
   - Ⓒ pull
   - Ⓓ push

3. What word describes how fast something moves?
   - Ⓐ force
   - Ⓑ distance
   - Ⓒ gravity
   - Ⓓ speed

4. What are pushes and pulls?
   - Ⓐ forces
   - Ⓑ balls
   - Ⓒ air
   - Ⓓ wagons

Draw lines to match the words to their meanings.

backward •   • a round object that turns

distance •   • moving from one place to another

force •   • toward the back

forward •   • to bring an object closer

gravity •   • something that makes an object move

motion •   • to move an object farther away

path •   • how far an object moves

wheel •   • how fast something moves

pull •   • the force that pulls everything down

push •   • toward the front

speed •   • the distance and direction that something travels

Unit Review

Visual Literacy

What Is Happening?

Daily Science

Big Idea 6

WEEK 5

Look at each picture. Read each sentence.
Circle the sentence that matches the picture.

1. Gravity makes the ball come down.

Gravity makes the ball go up.

Gravity makes the ball go fast.

2. The car is pulling the boy.

Gravity is pushing the car.

The boy is pushing the car.

3. The rocket will go slow.

The rocket will go fast.

The rocket will not go.

4. The ball will go far.

The ball will go in a circle.

The ball will not go anywhere.

Forces on the Playground

Think about how you play on a playground. How do you use pushes and pulls?

What You Need

• a pencil or crayons

1. Go outside and play on a playground.

2. Write or draw three things you did on the playground. Then write whether each thing was a push or a pull.

What I did	Was it a **push** or a **pull**?